T0099600

**A South Side Girl's
Guide to
Love & Sex**

A SOUTH SIDE GIRL'S GUIDE TO LOVE & SEX

POEMS

Mayda Del Valle

TIA CHUCHA PRESS

Copyright © 2018 by Mayda Del Valle. All rights reserved.
Printed in the United States.

ISBN: 978-1-882688-56-2

Book Design: Jane Brunette
Cover art: Mayda Del Valle

Grateful acknowledgement is made to the Northwestern University Press Drinking Gourd Chapbook Series for publishing The University of Hip Hop in which some of these poems originally appeared.

Published by:
Tia Chucha Press
A Project of Tía Chucha's Centro Cultural, Inc.
PO Box 328
San Fernando, CA 91341
www.tiachucha.org

Distributed by:
Northwestern University Press
Chicago Distribution Center
11030 South Langley Avenue
Chicago IL 60628

Tía Chucha's Centro Cultural & Bookstore is a 501 (c) (3) nonprofit corporation funded in part over the years by the National Endowment for the Arts, California Arts Council, Los Angeles County Arts Commission, Los Angeles Department of Cultural Affairs, The California Community Foundation, the Arts for Justice Fund, the Annenberg Foundation, the Weingart Foundation, the Lia Fund, National Association of Latino Arts and Culture, Ford Foundation, MetLife, Southwest Airlines, the Andy Warhol Foundation for the Visual Arts, the Thrill Hill Foundation, the Middleton Foundation, Center for Cultural Innovation, John Irvine Foundation, Not Just Us Foundation, the Attias Family Foundation, and the Guacamole Fund, among others. Donations have also come from Bruce Springsteen, John Densmore of The Doors, Jackson Browne, Lou Adler, Richard Foos, Gary Stewart, Charles Wright, Adrienne Rich, Tom Hayden, Dave Marsh, Jack Kornfield, Jesus Trevino, David Sandoval, Gary Soto, Denise Chávez and John Randall of the Border Book Festival, Sandra Cisneros, Luis & Trini Rodríguez, and others.

CONTENTS

2
A Southside Girl's
Guide to Love & Sex

Coda

FOR ALL THE
SOUTH SIDE GIRLS

Call Water, Call Agua

spill omi to call agua
spill omi to call iya agua

rock the body
let the shoulders undulate rain
like, movement made in mourning

the feet pound drum beat
white flowers, watermelon, molasses,
seashells hold her sound,
starfish gaze
deep, her night and morning

whisper of wet in ear
fog foam drops,
grows into her roar, tides
moves ache out the heart,
washes hurt from the chest
past off the hands
moves calm into belly
cleans, clear, crystalline, like
omi agua water

head fills with wet
head fills with omi
head rocks   shoulders
chest and legs move
like omi

let hands call
let feet spell
let mouths call
     omi ooooooooooo
     omi ooooooooooo

mami spread your skirt
omi agua water
over the parch of this concrete angel
fill the cienegas and canyons
green again

     omi ooooooooooo
     omi ooooooooooo

iya carry us home,
omi agua water
back to ourselves
across the seas,
held precious
in the shelter of your palm

water to call
we call
water to call
we call

the mother of fish
water we call
iya
the madre of clouds
water we call
iya

the madre who washes the path
iya who feeds humankind
madre connecting the continents
madre protecting our crossing
iya who yields the rain sword
madre who wears the silver crown
iya who beholds her beauty in the mirror
iya who lives in the deep omi
mother who fills all the dry spaces
mother who moistens what we've hidden

iya who heals
madre renews
madre who heals
iya who holds
iya protects

iya mother madre
       omi ooooooooooo
       omi ooooooooooo

water to call water
we call,
water to call water
we call water,
iya, mother, madre
we call water
iya, mother, madre
           we call water

1

THE UNIVERSITY
OF HIP HOP

Chicago, c. 1993

Mix Tape As Ars Poetica

back in the days
when i was young i'm not a kid anymore
but some days
i sit and wish i was a kid again
                                    —Ahmad

Original Mix:

We'd roll together me and my people
always together
tight-knit like wool sweaters
with dreams of making it
big in our city—or making our city big.

Squeezed into the back of an '86 light blue hooptie
Honda Civic who's bumper we'd sometimes retrieve
a block or two behind us—still

The kicker box stuffed into the back trunk
bumping *Illmatic* and *Ready to Die*
made us feel like we was the shit.

On our way to see Common, live,
before he lost the sense,
we'd roll northward–kings and queens of Chicago's South Side planet
'cause anyone who's ever been there knows
it's a whole other world.

Cut:

People drive past us on Lake Shore Drive
witness to the antics of teens
who've discovered that weed makes weekends
with difficult parents easier to stomach.

Their scowling brows take in the pants sliding off our asses
oversized T-shirts clinging to our shoulders
staring at us like   outer space
reminding us
            You're lucky you get to go out at all. When I was your age...

We wave off their admonishments
make out in the back seat while friends drive us to the mall
later hiding hickeys with turtlenecks
or trying to twist them off with a cold lipstick top.

Cut:

Spray can in one hand bottle of cheap liquor in the other
backpacks and fat laces
we swore we'd rep the Chi for life
carry the rhythm of fat caps, funk, skateboards, and turntables.

I pull my skully with the brim low
pull up my men's size 32 jeans
and bob my head to this, my era of hip-hop.

Break:

I reminisce on the cipher of familiar faces.

Rewind:

Hitting up the corner store
we trade our Saturday nights and fake ID's
for bags of Swedish fish and Cool Ranch Doritos
buying cheap bottles of Boones and margarita mix.
We gather every weekend to let the smoke
of hand-rolled jays wander across our faces
like clouds across our city's skyline
during summer thunderstorms.

We gather in that cipher
six or seven deep with a deep-dish

pizza from Palermo's
a twelve pack of icy RC colas
and watch *Style Wars* or *Beat Street*
dreaming we'd travel to New York
bomb train yards like it was still back in the day.

Remix:

We were so new school
worshipping anything
that anchored our devotion
to hip-hop in authenticity.
We were in love
with a culture that gave us the space
to rebel against our parents' blue collar dreams.
In love with music that gave us reason.

After a few rounds of passing the jay
and once the *Style Wars* tape starts
to rewind itself in the VCR
we roll
downtown into the loop
with nothing but the clothes we racked from Marshall's
the paint we racked from True Value
and the names we picked—

Scratch:

meela	peas	side 2	acter
bigs	noble	vegas	sam one
sleek			

Cut:

We sneak into subway tunnels,
slink like rats that claim the underground
and emerge
with paint-dripped shell toes,

cold noses, and fingers
turned aqua black and pink

run on the El tracks
suspended above the below
zero streets of Chicago
wishing we were suspended in time.

Blessed with the cockiness and certainty of being sixteen
we believed we ran the city.

Scratch:

Before the broken hearts
before the reality of bills and student loans
before the reality of Enfamil and Pampers
before the now and later sweetness of our youth
we existed within that cipher of familiar faces
with hip hop as our soundtrack
and fear never factored into our futures

cause

Timeline

1978
Latex can fail.

1979
Carter.

1980
Red flowers white dress. Buster Browns. Screen Windows. Bangs. Lace
socks. That lady who always sings too loud and nasally at church.

1981
St. Basil. Easter mass. Handmade dresses and bonnets. Frankincense
gold chain swing, red and white altar boys, cheeks poked
like ripe avocados.

1982
A-E-I-O-U and sometimes Y. The Cuban neighbors husky Natasha has
one blue and one green eye.

1983
Bowl cut. Corduroy overalls. Christmas Pageant school gym.
Big brother white navy hat and uniform visits.

1984
White people everywhere. Priests tongue foreign. New nuns in school.

1985
Sorry Jesus for talking in class. Wood planks leave lines in knees.
Shame feels like a bowl of hot soup in your belly.

1986

Snow-white lily winter day. A closet tastes inappropriate in her mouth.

1987

Rice Krispy Treats, bake sale cookies.

1988

Perms smell crazy.

1989

Berlin. No Saturday morning cartoons.

1990

Ibuprofen alleviates abdominal pain.

1991

First kiss: way sloppier than I thought.

1992

Maria High School. Bigger buildings. Room numbers. New uniforms.

1993

The bathroom is the perfect place to hide from boys who ask me
to dance.

1994

Ready to Die. Illmatic. Gin and Juice. Bomb The Suburbs. 36 Chambers.
A smoke filled 84' Honda Civic.

1995

A small red bloom gives me a shit-eating grin at Thanksgiving Dinner.

1996

Lots of white people. Again. Ivy-covered buildings. Count brown faces and miles from home. Stubborn refusal to call a cramped dorm room *home*.

1997

The city starts to slip off the tongue but the academy does not find footing on the palate.

1998

Prodigal daughter island humidity return. Old women recognize the mother written on the face and in the smile.

1999

Africa. Durban. First sunburn below the equator. More brown faces than I have ever seen.

2000

Caps and gowns. New city home. Chino Latino restaurants. Spanish Harlem. Subways that run all day and night. Apple Martinis. The Nuyoricans Creaky floor. Poems. Words. Microphones. Hosts. Lists. The 1st rent check.

2001

House Fire. Everything covered in soot. Furniture, books, clothes. Nothing turned to ash. Just soot. No security deposit returned.

2002

Poems. Poems. Poems. Delivered in a dark Broadway theatre. Rita Moreno stood right here.

2003
The Grind. One day off a week. Eight shows a week.
Sore throats. Poems. Bronchitis. Poems. Fever. Poems. Pulled muscles.
Poems.
Delivered in a dark theatre.

2004
Tour. A new city everyday. Every week. A suitcase carries home.
Hotel rooms all smell the same. Unless it's a five star.
ORD has the best bathrooms.

2005
A new city.
A new lease.
A cliché lover.
An old story.

2006
L.A. L.A. No seasons.
All sun all day.
The dead visit my dreams in L.A.

2007
Heineken changes the tone of his voice.

2008
That damn rent check.

2009
A decade later. Island return on my terms. Santurce sunrise.
La Respuesta on Monday nights.
B-boys Boricua style. Medallas and chichaitos.

2010
Second island return on my terms.
Consider this: 85 degrees every day. Beach every day.
Leave behind another cliché lover and make the floating rock home?

2011
L.A. The solitude is startling.

2012
This lover considers buying me an emerald ring.
Small hands small fingers.

Back Window

I am 8, staring out the back
window of my daddy's Chevy
on a Saturday afternoon down 71st St.
before it became Emmett Till Road.
Black dots hover in the sky,
sound and chopped air engulfs the car.
Before my tongue can even wrap around these syllables,
before my mind can wrap around their meaning, I see
the wave of red, black, and white flags, swastikas,
shirtless skin heads, KKK emblazoned on chests, combat boots
and black leather clad shoulders, visible between the wall
of blue: silver badges and night sticks,
police cars and restless horses enveloping Marquette Park.
Hear that word my ma told me I should never use,
see it printed, black and bold on poster boards
held high:

This is America.

This is How You Leave Home

It's not that I hated home—
it's just that my sense of destiny made me look
beyond the invisible border.

The night before I left for college,
my cousin Edgar married his HS sweetheart Rocio.
The coral dresses my sister and I wore were just like
the ones we wore a week earlier for her best friend Delilah's wedding.
My mother wished we just recycled those damn dresses—
no one would have known the difference.

Rocio's youngest brother looked at me all night
like he wished we'd met sooner
and when I saw him a year later on a trip home
when my sister was dating his older brother
his gaze slipped up and down the extra freshman fifteen
that had settled in places that bordered on adolescent
the last time he saw me.

Anyway—

we left the reception early, came back to the house to finish packing.
Already in the backseat were the green Samsonite
suitcases we used for that trip to Puerto Rico when I was five,
boxes with my twin-sized bedding, my favorite stuffed animal,
jammed up next to the dorm-room-sized fridge and small TV
with built-in VCR that they got me from Service Merchandise.

I took off the coral taffeta, looked around the wreck of my room:
the white canopy frame that I'd slept under since I was three,

taken apart and put downstairs, so I could leave the mattress
on the floor, attempt to have a grown looking room.

That was last summer, the last time I ran up to the sweltering cathedral
cavern of our attic, swung out the windows so I could stick my head out,
just to catch a glimpse of downtown, far out in the distance.
I could see the sparkling outline of the Sears Tower and the John Hancock.

When we got on the I-90 heading east to Indiana I looked back
to see the point of the Sears Tower blink in the distance.
Repeating my mother's exodus from her island birthplace
to escape from her mother. I inherit this tendency to run.
On the radio: *This is how we chill from 93' till.*

This is How Our Bodies are Made to Apologize

I was the girl who worked behind the counter at the skate shop. Never stepped on a skateboard, but could put one together like one of the boys. Grip tape, German ball bearings, Indy wheels and Shorty hardware with a grip tape cut so clean the corner barber woulda looked twice. It was just me and him on the morning and afternoon shift. I wore thin worn polo shirts I bought at the thrift store, 'cause the vintage polyester hung different, and thin white cotton bras that I didn't know didn't always hide the dark outline of my areoles. I had my hat on backwards. My men's size 33 Girbauds hung just right on my ass and my black-and-white Airwalks had just got a new pair of extra-wide fat laces. He approached me from down the counter, walked over to where I was to grab a wrench and looked down my shirt. *I can see through it*, he said and brushed my breast, and as his hand came back down I cringed and my shoulders shot forward, chest caving in on itself like a rose blooming inward. He stood in front of me, the wall of wrenches and shoelaces and skateboards behind me, and I had nowhere to go.

Mami's Advice

Kissing is ok.
Touching up here is ok.
Nothing lower
        Keep your legs closed.
Learn how to cook if you want to get married.
Cover the rice with two finger-widths of water.
If you don't put enough oil in the caldero,
you won't get pegao.
        Keep your legs closed.
Why buy the cow....
Clean everything,
not just what your suegra sees.
It's good to pray a rosary every once in a while.
Don't step on ants just because you can.
        Keep your legs closed.
Separate whites, colors, and blacks.
Socks go separate.
Wash your *pantis* in the shower
if you have an accident during your regla
before putting them in the wash.
        Keep your legs closed.
Close the windows, the dust will get in.
Boil a pot of water with cloves after frying chicken
to get rid of the smell.
Iron this material inside out so it doesn't get shiny.
Cross your legs.
        Don't keep 'em open like that.
Turn the fire down on the rice once the water burns off.
If you add water while you're cooking make sure it has salt.
Put the aluminum foil shiny-side down.

Keep the lid on tight and
      keep your legs closed.
It's better to water plants early in the morning,
If you water them at night you'll get slugs,
They'll eat your plants y te la matan.
But you can use a saucer full of beer,
They'll crawl in and drown.
      Keep your legs closed.
Always take an envelope with something in it to church.
Make enough food in case someone drops by.
Eat the leftovers.
Don't keep the fridge open, penguins don't live here,
close it and
      keep your legs closed.

After School Special

There was the blue hoopty,
always the blue hoopty.
Maybe it had a name
I don't remember. Let's call it—
Electric Youth
The Blue Avenger
The Blue Star.
I do remember the radio wires poking out
like stubborn metal hair, hand rigged to the kicker
box in the trunk Joe had bought that summer
on Maxwell street in Jew town
when he suddenly came up on some extra money.

The Blue Bullet. A home of sorts;
make out nest, weed den,
strategy room, storage space
for spray cans, rolled up linoleum
and Puma windbreakers.
A sputtering stallion of duct tape
and cassette mixtapes
on Maxell magnetic ribbons
the chill spot on wheels
where we steady stayed sinnin'.

Joe picked me up after school.
Maybe I lied about having theatre rehearsal
or a French Club meeting
maybe I used 25 cents
on the payphone we weren't supposed to use
during school hours
and left the 911 code on his beeper.

Whatever—

We sat in the safety of the blue Honda.
September, October maybe
when the last ghosts of summer cling
to the rains that pull down the first
leaves of fall shrouding themselves
in flashes of gold and rust.

In Marquette park,
always the park
where we made out after dates at Gertie's
for chili dogs and ice cream

and there was a song
always a song on the radio
Pharcyde just dropped

> *Can't keep running away*
> *Can't keep running away*
> *Uh one, two... so listen here...*
> *There comes a time in every man's life*
> *When he's gotta handle shit up on his own...*

One—

windshield wiping rain
water and catholic school
fear condensing on the inside of the windows.

Two—

my period's late and
my mom asked me if I was pregnant this morning.

So listen here:

I don't remember the words exactly
just that we weren't having sex yet.
Just virginal dry humping.
But legend had it
according to someone's sister
or cousin, or that creep-ass greasy teacher in room 208
that if you dry humped hard enough
one rogue sperm could work its way
through two layers of underwear
and get you pregnant—
an immaculate conception.

And there I was
16 and scared, a shroud
leaf shaken from its tree
and wanting to run
and I believed it all—
believed my mothers accusatory stares
believed the body that was betraying me
with an irregular period
believed the nuns and teachers who considered us all
hormone-ravaged daughters of Eve.

And I had seen what happened to pregnant girls at school.
How they were suddenly no longer student council secretary.
How everyone stared.
How their eyes puffed red
swole on the regular
along with the belly.
How the diploma came without the walk across the stage.
How they disappeared without an explanation.

How my mother said once

  that's what they deserve
  for betraying their parents
  and the Catholic Church.

The Wolf River

That summer before junior year of High School
all city slicker attitude, house music, and skunk weed
me, my boyfriend Joe, my homegirl Ingrid,
and Dario rafted the Wolf River.

We were warned by a tribal elder—
the wolf always takes something.

But what the fuck did we know about appeasing elemental
spirits? What did we know about ancestors?

So we paddled down river with bravado and a sack of weed,
cracking jokes the whole way.
As long as the wolf don't take our weed we're cool.

Then we forked to the left, instead of the right,
got tossed out of our cobalt rubber rafts
like coins into the rapids, lost our paddles,
tried to bail the water while flapping around
in tangled tree roots that reached for our feet in the dark water

When we shot over a waterfall
we reconsidered the wolf.

Back on the steady of the shore, we took inventory.

Someone lost their chanclas.   Someone lost a shirt.
         Someone lost their keys.

My sunglasses were gone.

                    What about the weed?

Joe held up a soggy Ziploc.

Do you think it's real?

Do you think the river knows what to take?

That night we snuck into the boys' room

and let the smoke float out the window

carrying our nervous laughter and awe.

Why you talk like that?
or the Etymology of "Where are You Really From?"

'cause it's a language of necessity
'cause it's translating for my father at the social security office
and my mother having a readers digest subscription for over 30 years
'cause i grew up on 64th and california
'cause i went to an ivy league and clutched
onto the south side
the way a hawk grasps it's prey
hunting the hood in my dialect every time
i came back home and the homies said
you sound white
right now
like
you not from here
no more

'cause you're so regional
you sound so chicago
and you speak english so well
how did you learn
'cause folks know i'm from where i'm from
when i say shit like pop
and drawl the caw
in chicago
'cause i got a lineage
of brujas sing-songin'
their black cat
callin' conjurations caught on my incisors
'cause i code switch between magic and academic
'cause i coño carajo me cago en na'

feel like it
'cause oakland gave me hella even tho i never lived there
'cause que
porque
qué pasó
qué hace
nada
quién eres
'cause the world thinks i'm nada
thinks brown girls are nada
nadie
nobody think they gotta listen
so i extra lip smack
away the silence
with a head swing in spanglish
and muthafucka
fuck fuck
fania salsa
slip my way across this bridge i live on

This is How the City Began to Slip

I left Chicago eighteen years ago,
gone the same amount of time I lived there.
All I have are soft-focus vignettes of a 17-year-old girl.
More mythic than anything else, I dress her in memory,
the city veiled in nostalgia.

Like, the way my mother talks about leaving PR at 17:
how all her memories are soft focus vignettes,
chirping birds blooming tropical flowers, sunsets
and the light strains of a guitar strumming jibaro music
like some sort of Boricua Disney princess movie.

Like, the way her memory contradicts the reality of the island now:
bass-heavy reggaeton rattling
highways surgically slicing into mountainsides
polluted rivers and gruesome murders—

The city I left doesn't exist anymore.
The boys I liked are married with children.
The train lines we used as playgrounds
barricaded behind security cameras.
Sears Tower is Willis,
Comiskey now Cellular Field,
Gertie's on 59th a cell phone store:
Chicago is a corporation.

Our neighbors of ten years are getting foreclosed on.
Mad houses sit empty and shuttered on my folks' block,
red-brick bungalows staring into the winter snow mud.

My mother prays every day to get the fuck out too.
Every doubled tripled quadrupled utility bill
strains their Social Security pension income.
Every winter seems colder than the last,
every inch of skin seems thinner against the ice.

But I always come back like a prodigal daughter,
sometimes feeling like I'm from here,
some days thinking it's the only place that could ever be home
the only place that knows me.

Ode to Door Knocker Earrings

all golden and round
the way girl
all bent
metal circular crown
of flash
me queen
dangling from aural
bass boom receivers.
all hood
honey drop hoops.

oh precious metal display of ego!
oh golden calf circumference
of chingona chola confidence!
oh amulet incantation of my name
set in malleable metallurgical mix
of alloy alchemy.

i don't think they did my name in 14k

but fuck it,

i steady rock
the tarnish anyway
anywhere.

when i meet my creator
dress me in fat laces
a bandera de Lares
and my downtown LA

swap meet gold
weighed in ounces.

yea i rock the name my mama gave me on my ear.
yea i wore a white tux and gold bamboos
to shake the presidents hand.
and what?

gilded ghetto regalia
ladies first
regal steeze
B-girl couture
Louis Vuitton please.

the bigger the hoop
the bigger the—
the bigger the—
call me out my name

say my name
say my name
those that can't say my name
it's on my earring B
just read it

all gold all gold
all precious mineral
on precious skin body
adornment no delicate dainty
these my royal jewels.

Ode to the Chancla

Molded plastic strap spreading
like a slingshot across the arc of metatarsal.
Oh what symmetry!
What thong-thongthong-thong-thong
that creeps into the vortex of hallux and phalanges
and rubs my toe pit raw.

Two dollar K-Mart Payless wonder
turned Louboutin like staple
of I don't give a fuck fashion.
Oh how island fashionistas
bow to your hourglass shape chancla!

Oh summertime messiah
save the soles of our feet
from blistering sand.

Oh you flyswatter!
Oh you roach killer!
Oh you cobweb remover!
Oh you foot-fungus shower-shoe shield
door stopper, ping-pong paddle replacement!

Praise the form of foam!
The welcome cushion you offer daily
like warm bread to the calloused,
bunioned toes of tias and abuelas
who fling and flick you
fuacata and fuete
the faces and nalgas
of unruly mocosos and malcriados.

Ayyyyyy chancla!
Better you than the belt!
Better you than the hand,
the fist, or the switch.

Oh pliant apparatus of corporal punishment!
Rubber manifestation of intergenerational trauma
intermediary of family drama
the 7th styrofoam seal that makes you run
out of reach of mami's impending
          mira coño! get your ass over here
          before you really get it
armageddon.

Ay bendito!
What music
what rhythm
what chancleta
flipflopflipflopflipflop cadence
when you onomatopoeia your own name
with every polymerized latex
lip smack on pavement.

In the Cocina

mami's makin' mambo
mami's makin' mambo

In the domain of the Del Valle kitchen my mother is the dictator.
I refer to it as "Carmen's culinary queendom,"
She becomes a cuisine conquistadora
wielding a freshly sharpened knife like a sword above her head.
Here Goya doesn't stand a chance.
No pre-packaged shit.
She is the menu mercenary,
the soldier of soul food.

You need to back the hell up
'cause
mami's makin' mambo

She hangs the hats of iron chefs off the windowsill like roast-duck
trophies and laughs at the sight of any edible food item.

Mua ha ha ha ha ha ha!

No meat in the freezer?
poof!
Spam and corned beef in a can are transformed into virtual fillet mignon.
poof!
Rice cooks itself instantly at her command
and beans
jump into bubbling pots shrieking
"Carmen please!!! Cook me master please! Honor me with your spice!"
       Emiril and Julia Childs?
       mere hamburger flippers in her presence.

'cause
mami's makin' mambo

It was there
in my mother's kitchen
that I learned more than just how to cook.
It's where I learned the essence of rhythm and power.
I learned to dance in that kitchen.
Shiny aluminum rice pots clanging like cowbells
with metal spoons, cast-iron frying pans
the wooden mortar and pestle provided the percussion section.
With the radio humming softly in the background
the fall of her steel blade on the wooden cutting board
became the clave. The hissing of the pressure cooker harmonized
with the sizzling of sofrito and bubbling beans softening in covered pots
and her hands moved faster than Mongo's on congas during a riff
making mofongo con caldo.
She would say to me
       The way to a man's heart is through his stomach and your hips.
       So you better learn how to cook mija.
She gave me the secret recipe for ritmo

2 ½ c. of caderas
a lb. of girating pelvis
a pinch of pursed lips
a tbl. of shaking shoulders
and a generous helping of *soooooouuul.*
Combine and mix.
       This is the recipe for ritmo, and now
       I'm dancing the way my mother cooks.

Slow
Sultry spicy
Sabrosa

Natural
Instinctively
Drippin' sweet sweat like fresh leche de coco
Spinnin' as fast as piraguas melt in summertime south side heat
Dancin' with as much kick as cuchifrito and Bacardi
Standin' strong like a morning time Bustelo
Steamy as pasteles at Christmas
Blendin' my hip-hop y mambo like a piña-colada
my mouth watering for music
with sabor en caderas
soothing down my hips
dulce as Celia's
Azzucarr
Con dulzura
I'm cooking with sabor
I'm bailando con sabor
'cause

mami's makin' mambo
mami's makin' mambo

> *Mamucha. Come eat.*
> *The food's ready.*

Being Carmen's Daughter

Primero it's hablando in whatever language
fits your need at the moment.
It's stories about an unbalanced spirit-seeing
grandmother, about crinoline-ruffled slips
covered in Caribbean floral prints.
It's baby daughter to a baby daughter.
It's your best outfit and shoes made
to last more than a decade.
It's becoming a repository of family recipes.
It's laughter louder than everyone else
in the room, ghosts in the corner
speaking of the dead with reverence and wonder.
It's dreams about weddings meaning
death is around the corner.
It's Catholic hymns and rose-scented rosaries.
It's Virgin Mary litanies.
It's food and arthritic hands
pressing milk out ground coconut.
It's clean, it's bleach and mops
and vacuums and no dust and
"I have to go home and clean."
It's "Keep your legs closed,
don't trust anyone not even your own two feet."
It's "Don't depend on any man."
It's "I wish I could have's."
that bloom break and bleed
in unfulfilled, unheard possibilities.

a SOUTH SIDE GIRL'S GUIDE TO LOVE & SEX

2

What is the shape of your body?
(after Bhanu Kapil)

A
        clock
                ticking
a succulent
each piece
it's own whole

Aloe   barbed ridge spike
        sharp tongue
        seeping cool gelatinous
        salve
ginger
        creeping root stalk
        heat prodding earth

Yerba bruja, romero, llanten
a sprig of mint
        a baño

Tobacco
pungent smoke
coils drifting off lips and santos

A river rock
        molding water
sapphire contour
of a lake's body

To All the Boys I've Loved: Redux
Part 1:

I am not your mother.
It is not my responsibility
to raise you into a respectful being.
You have been weaned for years,
yet you come to me,
try to suckle my sense of self dry, wounded, and
half-filled with promises you can't keep.
A man too scared to stop acting like a boy.

I've become accustomed to sleepless nights and damp pillows,
become accustomed to waiting for my empty bed
to be weighed down with your body, heavy
with the scent and hands of other women.
Mornings with swollen eyes are routine.

I cheat myself out of what I truly deserve,
settle for less, sleep with the enemy.
Take the sting of your insecurity and
lick my wounds in quiet mourning
for the little girl I lose by the minute.
I tell myself I can love away your scars,
wait for what I give away to be returned.

For Real

Our first "official" date: a night at the contemporary art museum (where we got walked in on mid-kiss in a dark cafeteria), a late night snack at the Jewish deli you'd go to with your favorite aunt in a part of the city I'd never been to, and a walk to a surprise location nearby.

But first you wanted to talk, clean up a few things, because you wanna "step to me right." You deserve it.
For real.

So across hot tea and a bowl of matzah ball soup, you tell me you kissed my cousin 5 or 6 years ago. That was all that happened.
For real.

Also, you were hooking up with a co-worker again, (after a recent breakup with another woman you would have had to convert religions to stay with), but you only love her as a friend, that's it. And you're ending it.
For real.

En route to the surprise location I watch my feet moving on wet pavement as mist falls, a ghost's winter breath crowning the streetlights with orange halos. I glance at you, a vigilant side eye. You're looking at me different you say quietly.

I'm drawn to a small play lot, with the gate closed. I stop to unlatch it, and walk in past the posted hours. On the swing you push me hard, my stomach all butterfly and lurch as I arc in the air. On the seesaw, we teeter back into humor, cracking jokes about waking the neighbors, the cops coming to arrest the smart-mouth Puerto Rican with the white boy who'd have to bail her out.

The surprise you want to show me is a small coach house, just next to the park. In the dark driveway, you pull me towards you. This is where I was born, you say, my parents lived here and my mom would take me to that park when I was little. I lean into you and maybe the skepticism softens, thinking of you as a child swinging in a rush of laughter, and the vigilance yields thinking of my own errors and messes, suspicion suspended midair like fog, or the memory of child's play.
For real.

First Date: A Perspective

"My favorite place to look at the city is near here
by the lake. I'll take you." You said, before
a long kiss under a misty Chicago sky,
on a night in December that wasn't too cold.
But it was all over so fast, that I never got to see the city
from where you love her best. And I'm grateful for that in a way,
because strange as it sounds, the way you loved the city
made me look at her again, and I fell in love
again, with the city I mean, just in my own way.

And for months I replayed that perfect first date,
so well-planned and executed, so
sweet and unique, something special,
that you'd thought of, just for me, and I would wonder,
why we never got to see the city together.

Until I pulled your book off my shelf,
the one about the city,
that you'd signed for me, so many years ago,
and read the blueprint for the perfect date:
museum, deli, and coach house,
that you had already taken someone else on.

A List of the Gifts I was Going to Get You in the Order I was Going to Give Them to You
(and also some activities I had tentatively planned)

A windowsill birdfeeder for the window in front of your desk.

An 18-year bottle of Oban scotch delivered to you naked in a trench coat.

An assorted box of Montana spray paint.

Two dozen fat caps.

A dozen mean streaks.

A day spent pretending we both know how to write graffiti together.

A deep tissue massage and pedicure.

A Star Wars DVD boxed set that we could watch together.

A vintage Chicago Cubs starter jacket.

A set of wooden handled fountain pens engraved with your favorite
    rap quotes.

Six of your favorite journals.

A pair of Timbs customized by Mr. Wiggles with your name.

The rest of the hip-hop saints candle collection.

A silver name-plate by Mare 189 with your initials.

A dog that we would name Juana Epstein.

An epic blowjob during a cross-country drive.

A trip to Culebra that would force you to rest for 3 days.

A hike up the hill on my father's ancestral land, where you can see
    the Caribbean Sea.

What are the consequences of silence?

(after Bhanu Kapil)

Vocal chords that turn to dust.
A voice cut
into glittering vowels.
Books left to rot.
Poems left to swirl on someone else's tongue.
You don't get it.
You don't get it
       do you?
Your backward speech
smart ass passive tongue.
       Say it to my face
       and say what you mean.

The Work

So I was going to wait twelve months before trying to date again. Quite a feat. No men. No body. This seemed a feasible goal.

*

I'm stuck in the passenger seat of his little red Honda. No AC, no window working, mid-August, stuck with him and the heat. He's yelling: something about women and men, and men following women being unnatural, how he had done that shit enough in his life and he wasn't gonna do it again. I look out, the sun glances off a crack in the sidewalk and glitters with glass. No dull L.A. haze around the palm trees, standing dark green almost black against the silent blue sky, no breeze to sway their crowns of fronds and crows. A bead of sweat slipping between my breasts brings me back and when I finally listen again the car is moving. Forty-five minutes later he is still talking and I haven't said a word.

*

It takes 21 days to establish a new habit. At least that's the rumor. I make valiant efforts at beginning something new, but I remain erratic. I have this tendency to absorb whoever I'm dating into myself. Or dissolve into their edges, blur the line between boundaries into erasure.

*

I never saw my parents be affectionate with each other I told him. I mostly remember them fighting and yelling. I don't want that kind of relationship you know? I want to be able to talk to the person I'm with. The minute someone starts yelling, I just check out.

*

I need to new age the fuck out my life. I need to do "the work." "The Work" is an oft referred to life process in spiritual communities that involves any number of activities that promote some level of self-awareness, even if illusory. Kale juice cleanses, qi-gong third-eye meditations, master cleanses, channeling sessions where you might be told the spirit of a small boy named Little Feather sleeps at the foot of your bed, using essential oils as deodorant to detox all heavy metals out of your system, eating biodynamic organic vegan ice cream, using words like possibility, authentic, and commitment, or wearing all white for seven days to help align your chakras.

*

The Chinese herbs he said would solve my "liver chi" stagnation are still sitting on my kitchen counter next to the herbs to help "regulate my period." I kept getting the sneaking suspicion he was trying to get me nice and fertile.

*

I felt myself resisting the dissolving. Staying up late to fall asleep on the couch alone. Pulling away from him in the middle of the night so I could breathe. I'm hot get off.

Chi-City

He makes me miss you.
Makes me jealous the way
he knows your morning song
and curves. The way
he sings your sweet
water shorelines.
How your bitter
sticks to his tongue,
how your wind puts the husk
in his voice, your twisted
geometry is his favorite
puzzle piece.

Albany Park

you see I loved hard once
but the love wasn't returned
-Lauryn Hill

In the third-floor apartment
you jokingly told me
I'd have closet space in,

next to the bay window
you told your mother you wanted
to build me a window seat in,

maybe you are reading
a copy of my new book.

On one page is
the poem about my broken
pen. My favorite one.

You read how it wrote
lines so smooth,
so even, so unbroken
in blue ink,

lines so Spanglish
so Piñero, Cisneros,
narratives so
you
so Chicago
they turned the river flow
back in the right direction.

You read how it broke,
how I took it apart,
tried to fit it back together
again, but the pieces wouldn't fit no more.

The order of reassembly
fucked with the function
and now it still functions,
still writes,

but it don't click like before.
Some inner spring
or latch, lost or
stretched too far,
extended itself
over the silence
of a haiku's 18th syllable.

It still got ink.
So much to say,
still tell you,
but it won't retreat.
The ballpoint
stays exposed,
always vulnerable,
ready to write
you.

Sex: in Four Shades of Sound

1) Get the Fuck Out of Here as Fast as Possible Sex

a quiet snore mid-thrust
a blank silent stare
looking for the fastest exit.

2) Great, Now I Have to Be Nice Sex

awkward glances at the ceiling.
the TV flickers blue and white
infomercials blaring on every channel.
numerous trips to the bathroom.
the futile search for socks and underwear.

3) Satisfying or At Least I Came Sex

scraping clean a plate
of spaghetti that could use
a little more
salt   garlic.
end the night with
a pint of ice cream
and a late-night western.

4) Holy Shit Sex

a humming rush
like water in your ears.
reaching for breath.
grasping the earth

in a handful of hair
arching back into a
hallelujah
yes.

Cloudburst

You were too cloudburst.
Not hurried or rushed just
not able to stay.

Here in this corner of my home.
Here on this bend of bone,
this sliver of now,

I sometimes speak to you
as if there wasn't a corpus
of scripture left unsaid between us.

Still when we laugh
people watch and wonder
what holy hell of a hurricane
passed between us.

Habit
(After Duras)

Maybe home is not a place. Not a room or a bed. Sometimes I think it's in a detail. A specific tea I keep in my cabinet, a soap whose scent lingers on my skin, a particular way of walking down the street. Or maybe it's a habit like a notebook and pen at hand. An orange Japanese Jetstream: black ink. A composition book wrapped in pretty paper to disguise its ninety-nine-cent store look. Or maybe like having a man in the wings waiting. When I don't have a lover there is always a potential. Or at the very least a longing for one. Usually, one I can't have.

Feels like everyone I'm interested in is a shoddy replacement for what I wish would have happened with him. The I-think-my-future-husband-showed-up-but-he-never-called-me-back-and-now-he's-dating-a-white-girl situation. Didn't help that my psychic best friend had visions of our wedding and warned me to take it slow. That made me drink a whole fucking lot. Made me smoke a shitload too. Made me curl up on the couch: Did I do something wrong? Slept with him too soon? Told him too much about myself? Forgot to flush the toilet the time he came to the house? Did I have bad breath that day? It's been the tiny sliver of glass my skin can't push out. Three years now.

***

Drug of choice No 1.

Men, to chase away the lonely. Even now when I go home to Chicago I can sleep through the clatter and clanging of pots, the murmuring voices, but it's the silence that wakes me up. Sometimes it's too quiet.

When you have sex you're not alone immediately. There's the touch, the warmth next to you. Knowing there's something alive next to you.

Something that watches you. Something that reaches back for you even when there's no desire to share any words. No conversation. Arguments maybe, but there's a body. Warm.

But, I enjoy the quiet of morning here. There's a satisfaction to having this space all to myself, that things are where I leave them. Clean like I leave them. And sometimes, the thought of bringing a man into this house again gives me a little shiver. M used to leave his dirty socks rolled up in the living room. S used to leave a distinct film of grease all over the kitchen and a sticky floor. Grains of rice in the carpet when they didn't stick to his teeth or mustache. Crumbs that would stick to my feet when I went into the kitchen the day after sweeping and mopping. Sometimes I fantasize about keeping my apartment even if I were to get married. At the very least, I would want a room. All to myself.

***

On those days when the habits don't fill up the silence, or when the quiet sits on my chest, on those days I am afraid the empty side of the bed will always be empty, or on the days I am afraid of myself, there's whisky and weed. It gives everything a soft focus. A hazy rounded edge where nothing is too sharp. I smoked in the morning. I smoked in the afternoon. I smoked before bed. It helped me forget.

***

I like this place best when birds visit the courtyard. Crows, sparrows, hummingbirds, even a blue jay one year. But mostly the mourning doves: they linger.

They're the color of cream, or fresh pressed khakis, but their faces glisten with a tinge of opal, an iridescent sheen. Mourning doves mate for life. It's true. A pair made a nest in the tree right outside my bedroom window the summer I went to Puerto Rico for two months and almost moved there. I heard the constant cooing and sharp whistle of wings outside the window every few minutes, so I pulled the blinds open to see one walking in a circle inside a small pile of straw, grass, and leaves. It was eye level with me and I stood there for a while watching it, it watching me with one black eye.

Later I heard a louder flapping of wings and went back to the window. Two doves now. One that had been sitting in the nest all day circled, climbed out, and the other one stepped in, circled, and sat. We all looked at each other. And this went on for weeks. One dove taking a day shift, the other a night shift. But every time I opened the blinds, there was one black pupil in lustrous sand looking right at me. Alive. Warm. Watching.

I left for Puerto Rico before the eggs hatched.

In Black Ink During Green Tea

Am I a container big enough
for all this sweetness, all this love?

This is what I fear:
not being able to hold
all the love someone wants to pour into me.

That I'll sink under too much
love, that I'm too small
for all a beloved has to offer.

How far could I stretch?
How wide could I sunset
across the sky, if I were willing
to break out of all this smallness?

Imagine that. Being too afraid
to break into something so radiant,
into something so free.

Chronology of Sound

Jan. 14
The echoes of water drops falling into the tub and I'm alone in the bathroom
       reverb off the walls.

Jan. 15
9:14 A.M. The sound of planes over the apartment getting washed out by traffic.

Jan. 16
The crows at 8 A.M.
Caws. Black shadows crossing overhead, just outside the curtains.

Jan. 18
Dana's voice takes flight, an adaabo over the drums.
       Orixa nee ya nee ya
       harmonize her angel tone, I have to stop and listen.

Jan. 19
The hum of the air coming through the vents
       hhhhhhhhhhh.

Jan. 20
The flutter of pages on my desk when the heat moves them,
       a ruffle of paper

Jan. 21
The exhale of the heating system when the air turns off.

Jan. 22

The hiss the skin of my foot makes when it slides across the metal chair.

Jan. 23

The keys of my laptop make a different sound without the vinyl cover.
>More click and scratch with my nails.

Jan. 24

The breath coming out his nose when he wakes up and smiles in the morning.
>The sound of his smiling: *mmm*.

Jan. 25

Maraca shakes
>makes the sound of rain in my hand.

Jan. 26

The car door closes and I walk back to my car mumbling to myself.
>"I love you's" need to be said when doors open.

Jan. 27

The ringtone is called jungle drums.
It's an electronic samba that whistles and
e e e ee e e e
when he calls.

Jan. 29

If a smile made a sound it would be 17 yrs old,
red velvet cake, happy birthday songs.

Jan. 30

He *mmm*'s and *yea*'s
cuts and edits measures of music.
I can't hear
what's going through his headphones.
I fall asleep on the couch to the lullaby of his humming and *yeeeeea*.

Feb. 1

There is a close-up picture of our hands together someone has
posted online:
his hands hold a calabash and mine.
Shells sprinkle and clink in my hands through my fingers,
spreading them across the shrine.
I flick a lighter and place the flame under a few leaves of sage
that smoke and clear.

Feb. 2

Yemanja Festival.

1: When spirit enters
the music enters the ears.
Fills, amplifies.
My hands over my ears do not drown out
the drum's increasing boom,
the vibrations coming up through the floor.
My feet throb. A heat travels up my spine. I think I'm moaning
through the hands.
The voices asking if I'm OK
are far-away echoes on a phone line.

2: The rain is a quiet sigh

Feb. 3

My back is sore and the only thing I wish I could hear right now is the bathtub filling.

Feb. 4

6:30 A.M. The fairy bells of the alarm on my phone actually work today and I get up to write.

Feb. 5

9:45 P.M. Mike the bartender at Alibi. The perfect Old-Fashioned. Wu-Tang over the speakers is a welcome break from the folk music that was playing when I walked in.

Feb. 7

The days I don't hear his voice, the only sound that stands out to me is his voice.
Even my fingers sliding across the screen to check the phone don't make a sound.

Feb. 8

me curé / me curé / con la bomba me curé...
1:28 A.M. I fall asleep in the car for a few minutes and wake up to the muffled sound of drums coming through the windows. I open the door to hear the slap, *pra pra pra* of the primo. I play and sing for another hour, wake up enough to drive home with the radio blaring the whole way.

Feb. 9

1: I don't hear his voice today, and despite the traffic, the neighbors playing cumbias, John's zombie footsteps heaving up the stairs outside the living room, the house seems extra quiet.

2: T's giggle when I flurburt her neck and toss her in the air is magic. J's dad clicks camera shots. S says *ohmigod she really loves you.*

Feb. 10
6:27 P.M. He left a message. The heavy in his voice made me cut across the freeway and head Westside.

Feb. 11
No classes today.

It's been a week, and the pain in my shoulder shot down my arm last night like a hot knife. I think it has a sizzling sound.

10:45 A.M. I called to let him know I was dropping off the keys. We went to breakfast.

The clink of metal on glass when I stir in the sugar.

His voice is porcelain plates bumping each other at the table when he asks how I know for certain I won't end up sleeping with the ex again.

My voice cracks with offense. I know. How do you know you wont hook up with the Japanese lover again?

Feb. 12
1: Went to see Freyda today. My back cracked top to bottom zipper when she pushed between my shoulders. I hadn't heard that in months. She wooshes and breathes and urges me to let the sob out. I'm so fucking tired of all this crying.

2: The mourning doves are back! I heard the whistle of their wings and those sad, sad cries when they were settling into their nest.

Feb. 13
All hotel rooms have the same smell. The same clicking doors. The same beeping elevators. The same heater/air conditioners clack rattle breathe into the room all night.

Feb. 14

1: The plane engines whir louder upon landing. A rush of mechanical hums and rattling plastic.

2: Wine bottle cork pop. Paper tearing on the gift I got you.

Feb. 15

Gifted him a keyboard for his iPad last night. Subtle clicks while the sheets swish around us. A Skype call rings out, fills the room with the ex-lover from Japan. A sarcastic Happy Valentine's Day fell out my mouth.

Feb. 16

The phone hasn't vibrated with jungle drums today. Fuck. I miss the sound of that ringtone.

Feb. 17

If the burning in my shoulder and neck made a sound it would be the color of red wine. It got worse after the last appointment. Freyda will probably crack the shit out my back this Wednesday though.

Feb. 18

I wish there was an alarm that announced the arrival of the cloud. I can feel it coming over me, but I never hear it approaching.

Feb. 19

The pain has crawled over my shoulder and into the area right above my heart. I keep listening for the pops in my neck that might bring some relief but they don't come.

Feb. 20

Sometimes I wonder if the neighbors can hear me crying. The walls are so thin I have to bury my face into two pillows so I can have a good un-self-conscious cry. I'm optimistic though. I don't ever really hear people having sex in the neighboring apartments. So either they're sound proof, or no one's fucking.

Feb. 21

Today at Locke, Eric reads his poem too fast in a nervous voice. The line that stands out: *Just accept the fact that myself is what I have to adore.* I tell him to take a deep breath and read it again. Slowly this time.

Feb. 22

1: M has a *-th* lisp when he says anything with an S.

2: The kids scratching on their notebooks, a drum workshop permeates the glass windows along with the sunlight.

3: C came by with Sushi, who jumped from the couch to the sofa for three hours with a rubber toy he chewed to bits. His little face smacks and huffs then spits out the green plastic on my brown rug.

4: 1:15 A.M. *I'm finally home* he texted when my phone chimed.

Feb. 23

Three hours. The ex's voice droned on the phone about himself for almost three hours, when I was the one who needed someone to talk to. How the hell did I...
When I finally hung up the silence was a relief.
Now I know why that shit didn't work.

Feb. 24

1: 7:30 A.M. I am so drained I can't pull myself out of bed. The sound of the teakettle doesn't motivate me. Nothing does. The alarm gets snoozed.

2: 8:17 A.M. For the last I-don't-know-how-many years, an unidentified neighbor hawks up half a lung every morning, at around the same time, while a shower is running somewhere. I can hear it across the entire apartment whether I close the fucking windows or not.

3: 2:14 P.M. I cry to sleep on the couch. I hate the silence right now.

Feb. 25

Everyone was so tired in class tonight. You could hear it in their voices.
The monotone drone and stumbling over simple syllables.
During workshop there were so few responses the unspoken *I don't give
a shit* filled the room like cigarette smoke.

Feb. 26

1: 8:00 A.M. There is a peace in Baba's shrine room that comes from
the colors of all the different altars and the music he was playing
on the radio.
Salsa songs he found that were all about Orisha.
His block is so quiet. No traffic. No blaring speakers.
When Baba tosses the shells back and forth in his hand, they have a
hollow rattle. A kind of wooden shell, and the sound ends with convic-
tion when they hit the floor.
The gold bell he rings while he prays always pierces my ear.
Irete-Ogunda comes up as one of my odu's and he lets out a high
pitched "HA!" that was part surprise and part "I knew there was some-
thing up here."

2: The plastic wrapper on the Thin Mint Girl Scout cookies.

Feb. 27

1: The neighbor who practices keyboard and sings rancheras and
Mexican pop songs every morning around 9. I don't know if it's the
same one that hocks and *huuuccgggkgkgkgkgkgkgk*.

2: 12:48 A.M. The sound of rejection. Again. Fuck.
A tired song I can't seem to fucking change.
I make tea in the fancy tea maker, and it always sounds like piss
when I put it over the teapot to drain after it's done steeping.

My voice cracked while I was pouring my heart out.
I took a sip to keep the tears at bay.
His silence filled the room.

Feb. 28

1: 7:30 A.M. It's been raining all night and the gutter outside my window slapping water into the puddle that forms in the dirt is the most welcome sound I've heard in months. I worry about the mourning doves and if they can keep the nest dry.

2: 9:13 A.M. My neck cracked and I think last night's conversation might have helped.

3: 12:00 P.M. The wheels of my luggage grinding on the paved walkway. I made it through most of the day without crying. During my connection in Charlotte, Ashley called me and I was sniffling so loud telling her what happened, the guy in the seat next to me kept looking over. I could only turn my face to hide. I kept hearing the patter of the tears from my left eye hitting the vinyl on the chair. I didn't have anything to wipe it up with.

March 1

1:03 A.M. I've had the heater on eighty-six since last night and it's definitely not that warm in the room. It's the one thing about hotel rooms that drives me crazy. There's never a moment without that white noise. And it clicks every few seconds when the thermostat checks in.

March 2

The phone ringing. Chiming over and over.
People in the airport sideways-glance at my raised voice.
Ten angry text messages in a row.

March 5

I hate my phone, the way it clocks in ex-boyfriend jealousy, some bullshit with every ring.

March 6

The silence of my phone is a welcome space. Home girls call to check in on me. The lilt of a girlfriend's voice brings comfort.

March 9

Does numb have a sound?

March 12

Not even the sound of drums cheers me up today. Every *gun-pra gun-pra* irritates my eardrums.

March 14

1: 8 P.M. B is a force of nature. His arms wave red and loud. His hands knife the air on the razor edge of each word.

2: 11 P.M. The post open-mic crew from work comes over for drinks. They fall out listening to Walter Mercado astrology predictions in Spanish. Even with all the Botox, sacred beads, and wide-eyed wonder his astrology reading is on point.
Escorpion! Coje tu tiempo que el amor vendra a ti. Tienes que conocer la persona, tener una amistad primero. Asi el amor sale bien.

March 17

1: 8 A.M. The pots and shrines in Baba's room hum what we pray for. I ask about the recently departed lover.
Supposed to be together.
The fuck does that mean?
Peace and victory.
They can't possibly be talking about the same man.

2: 9 P.M. Darkness is a man's voice speaking of rape. It circles in and through the 20 people in the room but settles in the bodies of three women present.

March 19

Freyda says I'm standing up for myself. And that's a good thing. Being clear about boundaries.

No no no no no no no no no no no.

A sound women are too unfamiliar with.

March 21

Shitty sounds like your car trembling on the freeway.

Shitty sounds like the voice of your recently departed lover, on the phone, while your car is trembling, telling you your ex is informing people you've been *"hooking up"* with someone new.

Shitty sounds like your recently departed lover listening to you laugh as your car overheats and dies on the freeway exit.

Shitty sounds like calling AAA to tow your car two blocks away to the mechanic you were trying to make it to.

Shitty sounds like the mechanic telling you it's going to be at least $2,500 to fix your car.

Shitty sounds like the recently departed lover offering to pick you up and take you home, but not calling back until ten-thirty that night.

Gratitude sounds like your best friend calling you at seven and shouting *Congratulations let's get a drink! You're getting a new car!*

March 23

Car shopping was not what I'd planned to do with my spring break. I start to feel a growing sense of panic with every jagged breath throughout the day.

March 24

1: I hate shopping. I hate cars. I hate slimy car salesmen. Every car salesman I've ever dealt with asks me out for a drink. I say thank you for the ride back from the dealership and close the car door. At least the one at Honda is nice.

2) A five-and-a-half-hour staff meeting. It takes 4 hours for anyone to actually sound remotely honest.

March 25
Car shopping. Day four. My phone is ringing with ten different dealerships and insurance companies.
Exhausted sounds like snoring myself awake on the couch.

March 26
Congratulations on the purchase of your new Honda!

March 27
The recently departed lover hasn't called since I was stranded with no car. I finger the steering wheel of my new ride. The volume on the radio only goes up to 40. Bronx River Parkway sounds awesome on the new speakers anyway. There's no more bass rattle of a busted speaker from the back seat.

March 29
Today is the first day I sit down and write. The scribble of my pen on paper is a welcome sound. Overwhelmed sounds like a sandbag being dropped on your chest

April 1
The recently departed lover calls at midnight. You're in Tampa, half asleep. The jungle drum ring tone doesn't sound since you've deleted all his information, so you answer it accidentally. It's been 10 days since the car died and now he calls to ask how you're doing. Did everything work out with it? What did you do? Oh the other thing I was calling for, do you know of a poem, or do you have a poem, that I could use for this project and song I was working on honoring women.

This is definitely what a bad joke sounds like.

April 4

Tonight we had 99% women at the open-mic. An eight-year-old got up and read a piece about magic and dragons. That's the sound of poetic justice. I sang one of my songs and I danced, while the recently departed lover played drums.

I left his shirt, book, and CD's on top of his bag without saying a word. We barely spoke.

11:45 P.M. My phone vibrates in my purse while I listen to an all-female mariachi band. The lead singer is wailing, almost crying about a lost love. That kind of voice and pitch that makes the hair on the back of your neck stand up.

The recently departed lover texts: *You killed it tonight. You were great.*

April 9

The whir of plane engines doesn't faze me anymore. Wheels up on the red-eye to Durham. At least it's a direct flight.

April 10

Students at East Carolina University, all raucous laughter and questions. There's a poem about women's bodies. A poem about kung-fu. Questions about spirituality and sweat lodges. The sound of breathing deep in spite of the sandbag on my chest.

April 13

A car alarm wails for an hour.

1001 names

(after Siken)

1.

i call you first. the beginning. before all the others. call you what do we know about love at 16. the first secret i kept from my mother. the first time i lied about where i was going. a summer spent next to the phone. next to the boombox playing sad salsa by la india and marc anthony. a summer spent waiting for you to call from down south. the first time cheated on. call you the first heartbreak. the first let's still be friends. first take him back. first pregnancy scare from dry humping. first making love. first fuck. on an old mattress laid on top of milk crates. first condom. my first blunt. first high. first house party. my first infidelity. call you my first spray can. rooftops and newports. subway tunnels and ciphers. i'll call you gold nameplates in old english for valentines day. first late night escape from the house. i'll call you car windows down. hair whipping in the wind like lakeshore waves grasping for flight.

2.

i'll call you i'm too old for this shit and knew better but did it anyway. call you messy. call you something like silk. slippery words. a midnight sky made flesh. call you wild woman wanderlust. call you sacred skin stretched, tuned under your hands to conjure the gods. call you late night phone calls from japan that rang while you were in my bed. call you long limbs that wrapped around me at daybreak. call you how many women in this room have you fucked? call your name. a name i shouted. like celebration. a name meant to bring honor to his lineage. call you betrayal. a silence. your name acrid in my mouth. still want you and hate that i do. call you young. a boy. made from the sins of his father. call you a father. call you the spirits you said you felt in my house. call us a thing spirit called together. a karmic consequence. call you divination. by holy men. with drum and dance and sweat. with bones.

with shells. divination with holy water. divination with sex. sex like ritual. call you i loved you and will never understand why. call you the wail of a ladainha. the scent of geranium in my hair you said still lingers. call you a mourning. saudade. mi querido. saudade.

3.

call you ghost. call you motherfucker. fuck face. fuck face. fuck face. call you my momma put out the good linens and plates when she invited you over for dinner. daddy warned me about people like you. fuck face. call you windy. the city revisited. like a first love retraced. call you the city incarnate, the city made flesh you're never filled up on. hungry. call you hunter. call you hunting to pour something into that empty. be it jameson. be it sex. be it the hunt. you same as a ninja. same as daddy's paycheck after the 1st. same as a word that leaps off your lip last minute and you can't remember. same as mami's figure after the 3rd child. same as the picasso's shadow in daley plaza at midnight. smoke in a windstorm. gone. same as the breath of a thing dying, always leaving. student of every fine ass woman you see. master of none. master of illusion. same as a nyc taxi round brown folk, you so hard to find. call you cliché. always told me to write what you know. guess that's why you don't write about yourself. and if you don't know, now you know.

4.

call you bad timing can really be a thing. east coast. port town. my best friend. call you a mirror i see clearly now. call you i still had so much growing up to do. guess hindsight is a motherfucker. call you sensitive and passive aggressive. beer changed the tone of your voice. call you, she left you fucked up. made you think that baby was yours. the aftermath of disillusion. call you i tried as long as i could. maybe i could have tried harder. call you pencil shavings and stout beer. a moon bear and ninja.

ibeji like my grandpa. call you loyal to the bone. mushrooms at disney-
land. a hip-hop encyclopedia. the good-guy. a solid man. only when it
was done, was everything really said. and don't worry, i promised you
i'd never write about the—H cream.

Wood

I'm sitting at the table you fucked me on writing about you. You were the first person to see the slab of freshly milled pine that would eventually become this table. A man from Arizona, who cut dead-growth trees for a living, delivered it to my K-town apartment. A dead tree, cut, sawed and driven all the way to L.A. For weeks the scent permeated the whole apartment, all the way to my bedroom. A sweet, woodsy camphor-like aroma that would greet me every time I walked in.

I miss the way you smell. To be real honest, I didn't like it in the beginning. At first, I thought: *Maybe he's one of those natural-chemical-free type of dudes.* I must have caught you post-workout, because eventually I loved the musk, the sweat, and I'd bury my face in your neck, or the fold of your arm and smile. There were even times I would smell you out on the street, in a class, at a store, and I'd turn to look for you, but you weren't anywhere nearby, and did I tell you I miss the way you smell?

The first night you ever came over to my house, the slab was leaning just inside the entrance next to my front door.
-What is that?
-It was supposed to be a table—But I think I'm gonna get rid of it. I don't have the right tools; I don't know what I was thinking when I bought it.
-You should call my boy F, he knows how to work with wood and he'll hook it up for you.

So I got his number, and you were right. He hooked it up. Took this 5 foot long 3 inch thick piece of wood and made it into the most beautiful table that I'll always remember you fucked me on.

***

F didn't just "work with wood," he lived and breathed it. He was a full time carpenter, taking on side projects when he didn't have a long term union gig building sets. When I finally got the slab to his garage workshop, and we lifted it out onto his worktable, he took a deep breath in and said,

-This isn't pine it's cedar. I can smell it. How'd you get this?

He geeked out at the live edges, the natural knots in the wood, ran his hands over the grain and pulled off pieces of bark. He showed off the new sander he'd be using on it, and some other handmade projects he was working on. A set of handles for a small cabinet, a conga he was sanding and polishing for you. Before I left, I asked how long it would take and he explained:

-At least a few weeks. You know wood, it expands and contracts because of the heat and cold, and we're on the West Side, there's a lot of moisture here, so I'm gonna see what it does before I get started on it. I'll give you a call and let you know how it's going.

I told you all about it later, and you did that smirk thing, when you breathe and chuckle, and you smiled wide, but didn't show your teeth, "Yea, that sounds like F." I stood close to you to lock our bikes up together and caught a whiff of you. It was woodsy, musky, and sweaty, and it was a smell I didn't know then I would miss as much as I do now.

***

When F finished the table, you volunteered to help him deliver it. I wasn't expecting you, so when I opened the door, surprised, you smiled that no-tooth smile at me, grunting under the weight of the slab. It was simple and elegant against the freshly-painted white wall, and the three of us sat and admired it, drinking some cold beers while the sun streamed in the front door onto the table, lighting up the swirls of wood grain.

A month later I called F again for a second project. Nothing as sexy as the table, just some built-in shelves: metal pipes, with plywood pieces floating on top. But still sharp and clean and well-made like everything he made. You tagged along again when he delivered the shelves on an afternoon in late August, when the heat weighs on everything, only this time I knew you were coming. I went to the kitchen to grab some beers and you followed me. We'd just started sleeping together the night before, so while F was dripping with sweat, drilling past plaster into the studs, you grabbed me around the waist, pressed your pelvis into mine against the kitchen counter and kissed me. All tongue and lips and whispers. Everything was new, sweet, throaty laughter, and keeping it secret was fun.

***

"For the sake of the friendship" and because "maybe it just wasn't the right time" we put the brakes on whatever situation it was we had going on. Maybe it was too soon after my ex. I got wary after hearing someone say you were in a relationship. You denied it. Plus, you were "going through some shit" and had gotten all distant and detached. But it wasn't anything to do with the ex-lover from Japan who happened to be in town. You swore to me. You got drunk and hooked up with her once while she was visiting, but you were over her, you swore to me. It was the ex-wife. You were still trying to figure out how to get along with her, for the sake of the boys, because you were over her too you swore to me. You swore to me about a lot of things.

We hadn't spoken in a month, but somehow, on the night of my 35th-birthday-slash-end-of-my-first-semester-of-grad-school-slash-Christmas-party, you were there. A few people decorating the Christmas tree, a few sitting at the polished cedar table sipping wine, and you dropped down on the floor next to me, closer than necessary to play cards. Your hand kept lingering on my arm, and when you leaned on me bent over in laughter, I breathed in your familiar scent. So when the phone rang that night at 2am, after everyone had left, I knew it was you calling. A week later, after I'd gotten home from an uneventful date with a recently turned vegan tattoo-artist, we were in my shower again.

***

The night you fucked me on this table was the night you picked me up from the airport. While I was in Chicago for the holidays, something had shifted and we started talking everyday. It felt brand new, like before. Throaty chuckles. Long conversations where no topic was off limits. In the car, I leaned my head on your shoulder listening to the radio, watching the freeway lights reflect in the window and illuminate the outline of your profile.

We'd planned a perfect evening. A bottle of rosé, leftovers my mom had sent back with me, baking a batch of fresh cookies, listening to music; a playlist called "Makeout Sessions" that I knew we'd have sex to that night. We laughed hard, stared at each other for long seconds at a time like new lovers do, when you're looking at each other memorizing the curve of a lip, the shape of an eye, when you're hungry for their face and more. We laid down on the rug, kissing, all tongue and lips, fingers tangled in hair, and clothes. That night it seemed like we breathed heavier, pulled each other closer. That night it was sweet, and genuine. I mean genuine, in the way a thing feels real, when it's new, and you only see all the good pieces. I trust you, you whispered in my ear. And I believed you, at least I wanted to believe you. That night, something in the timbre of your voice, about the way the Christmas tree and the lights up long past the holidays were making the room glow red and pink, something about the way our bodies fit together, how the music I'd curated into the perfect playlist crescendoed at the right moment, something about the quiet, the warmth, our skin sliding against each other, your rough hands on the small of my back, my back on the hard of the cedar table, something about how beautiful and right it felt, made me believe you in that moment. Something about that made me think he's telling the truth and he does want me, he does trust me. And I trusted you back, at least I wanted to trust you. And I thought there was nowhere else I wanted to be for a long time, here in the glow, your head on my chest, the sound of our breathing. And there was a quiet peace in that moment, something I thought would happen over and over again.

***

I don't ever write my lovers this detailed. I don't remember enough. But there's a picture of you I wish I still had. It was a Sunday afternoon in September. Just after the table, and the shelves. Before the silence. You had spent the night, and we'd slept curled around each other like quotation marks in my bed under cool sheets. That morning, we drove in separate cars to Baba's spiritual service, and I sat across the room because it was new, and it was a secret. You were drumming, and I kept looking at you out the corner of my eye thinking how your lips and your tongue had been on me just that morning. I kept thinking about the thick callouses on your hands, how on the days when you'd have to drum for hours, pieces of hardened skin would lift and peel off. I kept feeling the rough of them on the small of my back and my cheeks when you'd grab my face to kiss me.

But that afternoon, of the picture I wish I still had, you were sitting in a chair, working on a song while I tried to read on the couch. I pulled out my phone instead, waiting to get the perfect picture of you. You were dressed in all white, on a white chair, white curtains blowing behind you. Your hair hung past your shoulders and it moved like a curtain of vines over your face while your head bobbed, that soft smile on your face. Your shoulders and limbs spread out like dark amber branches, all grace, long fingers, picking at the air engrossed in the sound. Not noticing me, or the camera. Not paying attention to anything but the chop of the drums. Dam. You were the most beautiful thing I'd seen. You looked up and smiled wide at me holding out the headphones.

-Listen to this.

I wonder if you think of me when you listen to that song, like I think of you sometimes when I sit at this table. I wish I still had that fucking picture.

***

The night you fucked me on this table I'm writing at, the night I got back from Chicago, when you ate my mother's leftovers, and we swayed to music in the kitchen, I baked enough cookies so you could take some for your boys. Some part of me hoped that some time in the future they could like me and that I could love them as much as I was starting to love you. I think I wanted to show you that I thought about them, that I cared about them even though I'd never met them. That I noticed how light your voice sounded when you talked about them, how heavy it would get when you wished you could sleep in the same house as they did, the ease in your laugh telling me something silly they'd done. When a healer I was working with points out that I'd have to be ok with you having kids, I think how could I not love the children of someone I love? Why wouldn't I?

The day I met the boys I didn't know they would be with you. At a rehearsal, we were around each other, but not there together, and things weren't new anymore, but still a secret. The eldest gave me an odd side-eye, and a part of me wondered if somehow he knew something. The little one kissed me on the cheek when you told him to say hello, and later asked me to refill his sippy cup with apple juice. He looked most like your wife, because later, when it was all over, I found out you weren't divorced yet. Even though you swore to me that you were.

I think I really fell in love with you when I saw you look at your boys. When I saw the little one run and fling himself into your arms, and when I saw the way you lit up and didn't try to hide your smile. You laughed, so much joy on your face, I felt something pull out of my chest and get caught on the callouses of your hands. That part of me that got lost in the sound of our breathing together, that got lost in the music, and the Christmas lights. It's still there, caught, and I wonder if you can feel it at all. If under all that hardened skin there's a flicker, a small tingle. I wonder if one day you'll look down and notice a strand of light on your fingertip. I wonder if you'll blow it away, or ask where it came from?

Holy Day

Your tongue is a sacrament.
A holy I would fast for.
The miracle I keep cloistered
in the sanctuary of my mouth
an offering, a shameful confession.

But there is no shame
when we feast on each other—
Gluttonous, we baptize our bodies
in the warmth of a fragrant bath
in preparation for the holy hour
when we become a humming hymn.

The scent of our last supper
still hangs over the altar of my bed.
We are holy water
ceremony turned ash
tongue turned to relic
from the worship of skin.

Triptych

Moonbeams on the hollow
      Of your back
I rest my hands lightly.

You drift over me
      A feather in flight. We are
A dancing river

Melting into spring
An ancient song carved in stone
Waiting to be heard.

My Father's Advice

Slow slap of slippers on steps and I know it is my father. The familiar shiny bald spot pokes in: Que hace? Packing?

I'm circling the boxes in the basement of the house I grew up in, sifting memories, preparing to move across the country. I'm sore from a break up, break down. Yes, I say.

My father nods, then that long sigh that always comes before he speaks—

Que paso con ese muchacho?

> He had other women. He lied to me about it.
> I found a letter. That's how I found out.

Papi never said shit to me about men. Matter fact Papi never said much period. Calla'o, quiet. Shy, even borderline anti-social. Few words. Feo y franco.

But I think my father's reserve is more a kind of civility, a code of conduct that doesn't really exist anymore. He's a chronological anomaly, a throwback to an era when people knew what they were supposed to do and just did it.

Another sigh.

Sometimes, you have to be careful. People like that, they think they can take advantage of you. That's not good. It's not good to treat people like that.

It was the first time I heard my father imply I deserve something better.

Describe a Morning you Woke without Fear?

(after Bhanu Kapil)

There were hands.

      Cool hands on hot foreheads.

      My mother's hands.

      There was no school.

      There was light.

      A bright blanket of snow.

      A frozen water pipe.

      A covering of the city in light.

            A city in softness.

            A city that lay far

      beyond the window.

There were shovels and flakes on tongues.

There was chocolate

      hot

      sweet

      butter and cheese.

      Gilligans Island at noon.

      General Hospital at two.

There were dolls.

      Blonde Barbies one black haired Ken.

There was later

      the weight of him

      the heat of him

      the smile the morning after

      he stayed for the first time.

CODA

Daybreak

Morning with the gift
of languid limbs and lips
dawn delivers on her din of traffic
and the chorus of crows on
the creased edge of pillows
my feet touch under covers
feather light—
everyone should smile this wide.

Morning prayers should be
this hushed, whispered
as soft as our eyelids first flutter.

This is the time to set intentions
while our eyes are curved
into crescent moons.

Shout Outs y Mil Gracias

I WANT TO THANK MY PARENTS Carmen and Alejandro, for showing me how much beauty lies in being a decent and loving human being. My siblings Noel and Cindy for finding and rescuing me from the trash can shortly after being born. I am forever indebted to you for bringing me into the family. My nieces Olivia and Isabella, my nephews Nigel and Ezra, for all the laughter and joy you bring into this world.

TO LUIS RODRIGUEZ, a fierce supporter of writers of color who has continuously carved out a space for our voices. You were one of my first teachers so long ago, and it is only fitting that your hands and Tia Chucha Press are the ones to put this book out into the world.

I WOULD NOT BE A WRITER, or have had the success I've been blessed with, without the help and encouragement of some very vital figures throughout my life: the Southwest Youth Collaborative staff: Camille Odeh, Jonathan Peck, Jeremy Lahoud, Gillian Young-Miller, you put so much energy into nurturing our voices. Lisa Alvarado, Meylisha Sargis, I still remember your words and guidance. Sandra Burton, Kwe-Yao Agyapon, Marcela Peacock, you helped me survive four years in the purple valley and shared so much knowledge and wisdom. Dug Infinite for your friendship and influence on me as a young woman, you helped me look beyond the invisible border around the city. Tisa Bryant for your support and insight during my time at CalArts. Willie Perdomo for telling me to trust my voice so early on. To Russell Simmons and Stan Lathan, for the opportunity to share my work on such a powerful platform. To the cast of Def Poetry Jam on Broadway. The 9. I will always appreciate the nights spent together travelling the world in search of poems, and watching Iron Chef.

To The Nuyorican Poet's Café, knowing you existed in the universe gave me permission to write and to perform. To Hedgebrook, for nurturing women's voices and for all the space you've gifted me with over the years to take care of mine. An enormous thank you to the staff at Northwestern University Press and the Drinking Gourd Chapbook Poetry Prize committee for choosing my book and publishing *The University of Hip Hop*.

To my Oluwo, Kolawole Oshitola. You bless the earth with the gift of spirit and have helped to repair my life. Mọdupe. May Iṣeṣe continue to reward you.

To Earl Fasegun White, for initiating my journey on the path of Ifa. Ogun yee! I have been blessed with beautiful friends in my life who have held and lifted me up in some of the darkest of moments. Rana, Gigi, Cece, Nat, Kia, Sham, Ashley, Brenda, Myrna, Peter, Mike. Gracias. Street Poets Inc., for entrusting me with your young people and their learning. To all of my mentees, especially the young women at Camp Scott and Camp Scudder. You reminded me to walk with strength and dignity.

And to my beloved, Onifade. I didn't even believe I had a book until you told me I did. Thank you for all the ways in which you've nudged me to grow. For your belief in me, the time you have spent helping me with this, and for showing me that love always wins.

Mayda Del Valle is the author of *The University of Hip Hop* and a winner of the 2016 Drinking Gourd Chapbook Poetry Prize from Northwestern University Press. She appeared on six episodes of the HBO series *Russell Simmons Presents Def Poetry*, and was a contributing writer and original cast member of the Tony Award winning *Def Poetry Jam on Broadway*. A gifted performer, Del Valle has read her work at venues all over the world including the White House.